HUMAN
IS TO
WANDER

THE COLORADO PRIZE FOR POETRY

HUMAN IS TO WANDER

POEMS

Adrian Lürssen

The Center for Literary Publishing
Colorado State University

For information about permission to reproduce
selections from this book, write to
The Center for Literary Publishing
attn: Permissions
9105 Campus Delivery
Colorado State University
Fort Collins, Colorado 80523-9105. ·

Printed in the United States of America.

"At some point, or at gunpoint," by Norma Cole, from *Spinoza in Her Youth,*
© 2002 by Norma Cole. Reprinted by permission of Omnidawn.

Library of Congress Cataloging-in-Publication Data

Names: Lürssen, Adrian, 1969- author.
Title: Human is to wander : poems / Adrian Lürssen.
Description: Fort Collins, Colorado : The Center for Literary Publishing,
Colorado State University, [2022]
Identifiers: LCCN 2022037369 (print) | LCCN 2022037370 (ebook) | ISBN
9781885635839 (paperback) | ISBN 9781885635846 (ebook)
Classification: LCC PS3612.U776 H86 2022 (print) | LCC PS3612.U776
(ebook) | DDC 811/.6--dc23/eng/20220822
LC record available at https://lccn.loc.gov/2022037369
LC ebook record available at https://lccn.loc.gov/2022037370

The paper used in this book meets the minimum requirements of the
American National Standard for Information Sciences—Permanence
of Paper for Printed Library Materials, ANSI Z39.48-1984.

for m

home

At some point, or at gunpoint
Human is to wander

The light is not the usual light
The birds are
          —Norma Cole, *Spinoza in Her Youth*

CONTENTS

WATCHED FOR MUSIC

LANDSCAPE

to speak like one's mother, means to dwell,
even there where there are no tents
                    —Paul Celan, "Microliths"

NO LONGER IN A MOTHER TONGUE

l am his voice, she said in spite
of silence. A definition not unlike fire-

eater, half-brother, mother-descended
river. His lips concealed in mist. Tell me,

what does she do for the living?
In a game of meaning they glimpsed

self-conscious human nature—doubt
as physical posture. She could will her

self into his dreams: chair, child,
crocodile, shape-shifter with heads

of elephants. Eventually one might accept
these boundaries of home as given.

She would say bees or blood, he said.
Out of earshot is a river, she said.

And then a flood of newly acquired words,
snakes curled about a family name, ritual

of origins in the buzzing dark
of tombs, a child buried

and reborn. And in the corners
of her eyes: smirk of a muse.

Between *I* and *you* comes
a sounding out against

picture frames, chanting in exchange
for landscape. She spoke

as if underwater: Here
is a map. Here, a spoonful

of honey. Lying in wait,
the curious air of a genie

unhindered by voice,
she was indifferent

as smoke and driftwood.

His remembered fingers

volunteered into shapes on her
belly: goose, crescent, eagle,

hawk, firearm, rhino.
They were reading secrets

of a mother's young blood.
Meaning formed

in the darker shades
of an uncovered continent.

She engraved names
on slabs of clay,

a family music in
the imposed balance of finger,

fist, and feet, a process
of speaking without language

of prolonging lives
of animals in the delicate

etch and plunge and rhythm
of his unstoppable

Adam's apple. He spoke
but she was speaking.

CROWN OF LEAVES

as aphorisms
to comparison

so comparison
to shadow

plural of now
claimed just

before the shot
our captions

are picture less
each curve to the river

a bend in the light
is this a bird

or siren
to accentuate

invisible inside
the tree line

is he a bird
or soldier

bathed in pink
for a crown of leaves

who needs light
when you have landscape

who needs friends
when you have hidden words

like rifle escarpment enclave

like bluff

after Richard Mosse

FOURTH SONG OF THE CHILD SOLDIERS

Song for Hunting Herd of Gnus, Illustrated

Case of ditto for eating meat
Copper rings for arms and
Above the knee. Arm rings
Made from elephants' teeth
Ditto ditto for eating meat

Horn for holding grease
Many rings united
Ear plates ear rings
Case of ditto and whistle dice

Pick axe for digging
Needle and case. Necklace
And breastplates. Spears
Made from elephants' teeth
Ditto ditto for copper rings
And whistle dice for eating meat

PROCESSION: FIRSTS & LASTS, BY ONES & THREES, IN THE SCHOOLYARD OF GHOSTS

All I need is the sound of their footsteps
To tell forever which directions they took

—Apollinaire, "Procession"

I stepped up into the open doorway of a classroom. The dead
looked like pictures of the dead and even then

under a continual threat of being overwhelmed once again. When
pregnant women stand still, bathed in window light,

intently reading letters, where is one invited to imagine
the letters are coming from? Does a schoolyard really matter?

It was capacious, soft and reassuring; it radiated the same repose
we had observed in her face: morbid fascination of dirt, blood,

snakes, insects, smell, ugliness, deformity, size, and all that is grotesque
everywhere evident in the book. But we are warned that she has

premonitory dreams of attendance at the coming centenary
of the secret Society of Ghosts. Reaching the field, I watched our local

Interahamwe drill. They began shouting and waving their hoes around.
Birds everywhere as well as garlands, bouquets of flowers. She believes

in the coexistence of three different yet related worlds. However, I wasn't going
into any of these. Well, I am not going to. The more complete figures

looked a lot like people, which they were once. They did not smell.

DIAMOND NECKLACE

Three men walk into a question mark. Across the river, villagers waken to clattering as of drumming. Night rain on tin roof. Here, closer, an insect quietness, until eventually not even a whisper, and this is where the men (soldiers likely, professionals) slipped through.

Elsewhere a woman's ear is seen as the lean, lovely curve of interrogation. Smoke of a morning camp curls, too, over smoldering fires. But from far banks not much is visible, which is to say this history is hearsay. (Could be a movie requiring a tone tending toward emptiness, but for lighting.)

By lunchtime a decision is made. Build a flimsy boat: float a new village downstream to the scene. Tall men only in water. Cameras in trees with views of a helicopter distance. This might be sleep deprivation if in fact we are not acting from a script. (Movie as form of underwriting.) Ink in place for blood.

By now three men are safely positioned in a quiet room. Each has brought his own balloon, something a priest might do, or clown. Blow by blow they blow old air until the pressure of a new skin is just right. Now one ties a knot and gently, gently taps his balloon to rise as though by its own volition to the center of a quiet room.

Final scene: we see a well-manicured hand. (This also could be a television piece if it is in fact not a punch line.) Now an elastic echo, tap of fingertips on latex and trapped air rising again and again. For each hand-pat, the balloon rises and a dull echo. The boat will capsize; the village is lost. But first the last sound she hears: *Tap, tap, tap.*

THIRD SONG OF THE CHILD SOLDIERS

Song for Instruments and Empty Tents

We are telling the story of a cheetah elephant zebra and lion

They get nothing except the dust

They are fighting over who is strongest

You don't want to hear something like that

You can see the city from here but you can't hear it or smell it

Across plains punctuated by circles grass-ringed bald spots

A patchwork of troops and rebels covers every inch of earth

Each instrument cut to play just one note

Wire screen over cage to protect men from falling rocks

Black honey musky with sunlight and nectar

Bantu boys gagged for silence and

They laugh so hard they have nothing to hold each other up

Thin whispers of skirts and all minds focus on honey

You don't want to see something like that

We are reading a story about nothing except the dust

Each instrument cut to play just one note

Rocks are smashed and washed by hand

They are fighting over who is strongest

But how deep should you dig to maintain human success

We don't want to ask something like that

I am reading a story about thunder across plains punctuated by circles

I am living in my daughter's house

The thin whispers of skirts as boys trail their elders and

Each instrument cut to play just one note

Hunters descend with dripping combs

They laugh so hard they have to hold each other up

As boys trail their elders

They are fighting over who is strongest

They hide nothing except the dust

We don't want to know something like that

Thin whispers of skirts and rocks smashed by hand

Each instrument cut to play just one note

THE LIGHT IS NOT THE USUAL LIGHT

It's the pitch of the cry that carries
—Myung Mi Kim, "fell"

in which on
their heads

women carried water
and mountains

brought the sky
full circle

———————————

1. Or in what way is a hum a cry. Can it be a drone, a black box, a song. This junction agreed from the outset like father and son to conjugate a waste of excavations. Slips of the tongue adhere to scientific laws. "I could still smell the oil and ammunition and it made me." Many words should be amended, many phrases expunged. Troop or troupe.

count red pepper ticks
and ant lions
their countersunk

traps rain
pocks in fire ash
count soldiers' voices

hum of kerosene lamp
morning moon and undulating
sun rising in thorns

count dying
wind the coarse bark
of gray zebra

seized by our hidden host
over the plain
count oryx

fled into the earth

---

2. Encounter troupe leaving unheard damage in its wake. A child not only
splits a parent into two but he may also split himself into three. Encounter
flight patterns in which her acting career begins, in which following a ball of
yarn they finally arrive at ash: "We entered a forest and walked all night. We
found blood covering the path." Encounter drone sound song.

pluck red grass
spit in benediction

place upon the skull
when the rain stopped

the body would be left untouched
on the great Siringet

they have put aside
their warlike ways

———————————

3. Here lies a bicycle. Here lies a shoe. I could still smell oil and ammunition.
It made me back his argument with force ("time and space died yesterday").
Onto my head which ran the long neck and then into the pitcher in which the
rest of my body. An in in which words should be amended, family expunged.
Here lies a mother's tongue. Here lies an ear. The human shine. The hum.
Hum.

she heard death
willingly distance old

as recorded history
on this plain

the one great tree
would fall of its own accord

---

4. On roadways of nothing to fasten with, of the night before, of no one sleeps.
Of people sat down. Of parts of him with which he has now parted company:
slips of the tongue, smoked glass, ancient compass, broken saucepan, legs. "I
could smell a junction, split in two." Hum of bicycle tongue and shoe.

borders become
history or grammar

of doubt
passed from father

to son
yellow eye of earlier

generations
a chance to lay bare

eternal as fire or water
"Used to ask what sex your wife was—

probably still do"
silence and soldiers

negotiate the dark

---

5. Of everyone slept ("Is this a link or a hallmark?"). Of those with guns, or of
the Dada painters return to paradise. I tell you, before me is the market and
the death of the market: granite paving as clean as a skull, ball of yarn, noise in
the machinery of the brain, mother and child a human a hum.

dawn light should be rubbed
in a certain way

glazed with dread
from this journey

fire murmuring excuses
black-maned

lion in the grass
and over a triangular doorway

passage of night animals
to bless this pressing

transparent stuff against
the stream of glass as

whoops and chants
whoops and chants

whoops and chants

---

6. Laws of chance or an eye for rain. Many words amended, many phrases
expunged. They said he would go mad for one week, but I did not go mad
for one week. "I tell you, I was forty-five child ghosts of seminal energy
respectively, street by street. Street by street. Street by street." The human
hum, a drone, a payload, an ear.

AN EVENING LINE (I)

history calls for lines
forms and trains

How long would it take? You can only imagine. She is talking but to herself. No longer clear yet unafraid, as though by forcing it memory comes from the thing itself. And still some think nothing has happened. But what is it? An event? An experience? You can only imagine. Between departure and arrival all along has been this, and now she waits for someone to notice. It's as simple as an alphabet. She thinks. Up for grabs. Responsible to no one and nothing.

I am my own anthem. Her confidence measured now in tones. An old time borrowed from another song. Rare form. It helps to have a name. As fine a place as any to start, but really what she wants are five letters arranged into something resembling a hand or map.

What we don't know is that this all happens on her first day in a new country. A form of migration. She thinks. Neither necessary nor real. Stamps involved in much the same way as punctuation. Worth less with time.

And yet all of this happens before and is happening now. None of it documented. So precisely.

Meanwhile, close by, another thinks in his own way: Your hands know the right measure of care; your tongue is a gift. Your name a station between this place and that.

She thinks. All of it. Neither necessary nor real.

NEED TO PARADE

"What did you have in mind?" The men are finished and she is speaking. To him even now, one imagines. (This might be their story: "even now.") But to the camera he says, "Why? Why?" A lead role.

No one we know saw it happen—and the body lies except when it lies like history.

Earlier in the day tea from Malawi. And time. And for another thing, distance or a garden. But it lies in grass at the side of a road. To the airport of a course. (History at this time is "of a course"—reel, true as black and white. Which never is meant as funny.)

Watch it. Everyone said, after tea. (Everyone says, watch it, even after tea.) On the road to the airport the other mothers hummed "Song of the Child Soldiers"—a lullaby. The fathers stamped their feet in town. How are they keeping?

In time, reel history a distance and dance. But someone always believes a need to parade. Others call for beating.

Of bone on skin or skins. On tightened hides of slaughtered beasts. Of time, distance, or drums. One imagines. Even without a camera to capture it he might lift her wrist to show it was nothing. He is crying of course, that part is in the open. Everything is in time, even singing.

And a route carved in undergrowth never is a route for long. (The kind of thinking you might learn later, from television or history.) And even everything black and white has something to prove with distance. (This is what he has in the grass on the road to the airport. A longing, to say.)

But now she is framed by a reel kind of history without ever knowing it and he holds her wrist to wonder why. (This is what she has. In mind. On the way to the airport.) He knows nothing with time.

One imagines grass of course. And time like history or wings or beating. Watch it. Everyone says. Even. After. From.

A IS FOR ANGOLA

History is the learning of spectacular consistency privately and learning it alone and when more comes they receive.

—Gertrude Stein, *History or Messages from History*

Forever telling of another time yet only talking of the present . . .

—Yang Lian, *Thunder 8*

So the men went away, and the chief shook his head and mumbled to himself, "Nonsense like that upsets the community."

"Fantastic, isn't it?" his stool said. "Imagine, a talking yam!"

—"Talk," an African folktale

TEETH [A METHODOLOGY]

Absolute north is to guerrilla outpost as "love" and "antelope" are to the bush they occupy: uniform urgency as overt as names on a skirt.

The range is an exercise, tame as a vase, and to talk is to occupy. In time, the range is a plain without end, an envelope of light unable to injure itself. Or an ostrich, and light becomes the uniform—lips, a skirmish between what's open and what is tapping to loosen time.

The plan to explain is absolute, but only an entrance.

ACTION

An army and its camp. A tale of the interior called *Opening from the North.* The difference between rhyme and accent, rumor and a given name. The actual point to the ostrich in any movement.

Or when movement is the antelope and the tale is of an enemy always just beyond range. How yelling becomes planning, invoking becomes engaging, and noon is only a matter of time.

When what's left is a response called "home" and to be included means to find order in the rhyme.

ARMY

The accidental response of any movement, using yelling instead of creases as a means to exit. Or the outskirts of an enemy camp.

Something to solve, like a volley or love. An insect without a point; an entrance without a lamp; a door and, beyond it, an ostrich hiding a mountain. Explains a noun as an exit and names as a skirt around nationalism.

A way of saying, "You are tame as an envelope on the table."

BORDER

A band around what's open. The rational digression from "entrance" without rhyme, like an angle without a plan or the animal interested only in the net.

It is a harp sounding like a gun, the exit that comes from tampering, the group without a trace, their yellow dam built with nests of insects. As a response to reason, it becomes the story of the mountain and ostrich: an exercise that turns "antelope" into "envelope" and "North" into a system of names and actions.

Eventually it becomes a way to suppose that creases of light are the enemy.

BUSH

To see beyond the uniformity of sand to a new home and an old exit. Or, the way "nation" rhymes with "option" and "yell" really means insect quietness. It is the notion and the mountain—overt as fire—but, dismantled, it simply becomes an ending for names. It is the ostrich at the door, like a river without a message.

CAMP

A close amplification of mountain and persona, or the way lips move to the overt entry of an open palm.

The roundness of sand and loam—a national sand, an exit. The insect on the table, the open floor: really just an angle, a noun, like "yam." But the insect alone is not an angle.

No, that's a notion.

DEFENSE

The daily expectation of frames is an envelope—noun and sound—that enables action. "X" marks the reason, not the noble option.

Otherwise, what are noble are the insect and the paratrooper and their act of violence to uphold sense and urgency. The answer is land—an egress: a movement toward empty names. But mostly it is just the noon bowl of yams: a way to capture an excess of light in daily life.

Tame as an ostrich, its own exception, it holds the rhyme in "persona" and "entrance."

DUTY

Begins with delight and the ability to understand a talking yam. And this explanation of night by an antelope: "Sound the alarm, love is a desk with the light on." It requires a map to the interior for exercises without any prior knowledge. The group response is injury, but there is hope, like a season without night on a trap or train.

When the group asks your name, play dead.

FORCE

The feather at the opening is also a ring around a cause: to enter means to empty pockets of insects and arms. Noon is the action against the enemy—night, a way to say "uncle" or argue the difference between troop and troupe. The name and the gun: a system, like a river leading away from home.

"Expect the yam and you'll get the rhyme."

FORM

Exit the camp at noon. Find the rhyme in "hope" and "group."

GAME

When grass is absolute as a mountain, or when the excuse passes for the reason. When the box holds the option, and the x-ray shows the anthem left unsung. When the unit closing in from the south is just as much an opening in the north. When unified sound lasts without trying, and "skirmish" is understood as the antelope, not the enemy.

Expression is a form of training. Injury, a form of expression.

Neither requires a name.

KUDU

The knife and uniform always at the door. The urgency held in a name. A notion to occupy, or to range, decided by the difference between insect and inspect. Or, when "ostrich" is a game and "front" a feather without reason.

The inversion of exit and entrance: a form of overt nationalism, like the roundness of time beneath a mountain.

MAP

The moment the antelope enters the poem. That opening, neither nuance nor observation. The moment to treat the enemy as an exit. That enemy, no longer a mountain. The nation and its last team of overt personae.

That envelope, the one without the letter.

Mud and insects—or, the noon encounter. Whatever leads to an understanding of nouns as optional names.

A defense against sound and order, or the ability to capture an explanation from nothing. This "calling for understanding" is akin to describing time as "now" or timing as "an exit."

There is no other reason.

NAMES

The necessary actions to motion. Or, the English sound for "exit."

A camp, open as a noun, with an ostrich and the slow collecting of time. The taming of grass by something under it. To excel at inspection but have no interest in what loosens the neck or spans over it. The overt inside to whatever dismantled slip of night is next.

And always: a spoken antelope—a hope—a way of finally getting 'round to the yam.

NEWS (I)

A national explanation of war as solution, absolute as an x-ray, like an arm lying open on the table. And when the plan becomes the reason, it is the way light surrounds an insect and love fills a uniform.

Always, the route over and the angle between. In a time of names and necklaces, it shows how injury passes for accent and aptitude measures ox and oxen. Otherwise, it is a lamp passing for time, newly inspected.

Optional: it informs a notion.

NEWS (II)

The natural expectation of water and sand is to ambush—like an x-ray or anthem. It is not an accident of training; the plan has no training. It is a nest that ultimately ends without explanation. The door or roof? Nothing. Just a camp of remains. Here, the angle is to train without a lamp, to treat the accent as terrain, to look for insects in an open notion.

The natural outcome of reason tempered by a heart. ("Ample time to see what's under the envelope.") This extra element to time—tempered like an antelope and its moon by action that might be urgent—creates a cramped system for peace. The reason is a room without oxygen; or, an oryx and the elephant that tramples an armed movement.

Its true nature is a room without light. In this way, it remains an exit.

OPENING

The opposite of a plan. Or, the way an explanation surrounds itself with names. When "place" no longer means "land," and night becomes the offering, perfectly acceptable, for time on a train.

It is the ostrich at noon: neither necessary nor true but, like the rifle and hope, what a system requires.

This only difference between "insect" and "injury" is the sound of what's next (or "nest"), the way tapping becomes something to count on. The way "enemy" is to "encounter" as "envelope" is to "explain."

Close-range inspection of a front where light is not the entrance. An absolution of names without reason. Or, to inspect with a notion that names solve whatever remains open. This game to tame a group becomes a way to practice without nouns or hands. The range becomes an easy exit, a crease: something to trample like time.

It is what an antelope sees without trying. What happens to a national camp when one voice says, "Explain."

SAND

When the song becomes the anthem—or, when naming defends what's open in a notion. When "to answer is to exit" translates as "a noun gives time meaning" and the front is only something imagined in a game. It helps to find the exit, but to exist requires explanation and nouns and a mountain—and the familiar sounds of early words, like "elephant."

A system of killing that is irrational or rational, depending on the training. A way to say yes to the interior and make it rhyme with "answer." Or, the way a rhyme sounds like listening but really is just a response called "terror." (Not as action, as form of training involving a lamp and forced answer: "What is the difference between insect and inspect?")

To enter here is to initiate a total onset of night, as though the mountain were a noun lacking any real interest. But the night interests any group—the way an ostrich interests an antelope, or the way "now" needs "next" as its form of light.

It is a game of answers, this type of love.

TRAIN

A troupe following its rhymes, an antelope following its insects, the nightly reasoning that holds a nation to its names. How the need to inform finds opposites in "yam" and "time"—and how sound from a group is as uniform as a mountain. If to explain is to exit, then to hold is to peel (as in: "a fact")—but the explanation of love as "a camp held in time by sand and an ostrich" really is just another form of training.

Plain truth to the end.

Truth and the room it occupies. The optional persona in the anecdote about an ostrich and its time in camp. Place—and its elephant. (Or any lasting opposition to clarity.)

When truth is reason enough to kill and mud becomes a uniform insanity. It is the system that begins when planning is neither overt nor over.

The yam is a nuisance, but it allows naming as a form of answer.

Treason. The rhyme it occupies. A unit performing exercises for the right hand (piece called "Camp at Noon"). To be able to explain "X" but not "enemy" or "yam." Remembering to replace "insect" with "inspect" and "range" with "engage" before asking what moves a unit.

Time is framed by this response to sound—and so, the elephant scratching its post, the ostrich entering a cause only to be included.

Reason requires injury to become its own excuse. (The movement and its system, saved by an ending.)

UNIFORM

The urgency of a name informing the frame. The ostrich without rhyme, the mountain and its reason. It is an action at night, the ruined sound of a harp, that other game using movement and feathers. It is an action involving a train, or the yelling that underscores explanation. To enter is to observe, to repeat is a mistake. But the name at night is reason enough to enter.

The insect exists in time, closed as a mouth, clear as action. But the yam and the honey pot, the injury and the exit: just nouns.

UNIT

To say "uncle" but to mean "north." To turn national interest into a form of training. Or, when what's normal occupies a notion and what repeats captures reason in its own trap. How the antelope listens for the truth, and how the entrance informs the exit. How hope is simply the trick of rhyming between nouns.

The enemy becomes a song, held by time.

WAR

What the antelope recalls of heat. Or, how names serve at an entrance as accent, and tracks always lead away from camp. How tools become the entrance, like absolution. But the look of leaves, the ostrich, a single leaf:

This is the plan to exit without sound.

WATCHED FOR MUSIC

A man undergoes pain sitting at a piano
knowing thousands will die while he is playing
—Michael Palmer, *Sun*

I could list the parts of the body as in a blason. And
how they can get hurt.
—Rosmarie Waldrop, *Driven to Abstraction*

PALM-WINE SONGS FOR THE GHOST KING

Awe, Incantation

solar tell, gravity's homeless other

translated guilt heard our satisfaction

Gateway Horus, overpowered Sphinx to

theory: ghost-hurtle obliterates slope

shoes, timbre—gather heads out

his road to the future
reached a fork

primitive races drawing
sounds from reeds

or strings allocating music
to the realm of gods

he had carried it far
away before I woke inside this wood

ghosts smart to trek
short or long distances if they could

not bear the music
stand still then the whole

of them in intentional activity
in "doing" that these categories

are resolved—the body
which acts and has consequences

cannot be seen in dualistic terms
it works then naturally—he also believes

in something like them
only much more powerful

intelligent and reliable a guardian angel
will do so out in the world

years of belief in magic called upon
to compensate for argument no longer applied

with so many TV crews extracting daily
awesome images of death they were

to protect the living of course
but they fit the size of a dying child

Ore, Inclantation

our visitor has the quiet

confident look of one

who has chosen

to be she said

I noticed the silence of the house
on the faces of the guests

everyone on his best behavior
a keen anticipation where

the evil figure materializes
as ferocious animal

(it could not possibly turn itself into a little animal)

In those days without satellite navigation
it was much more risky than it is now

There were many attackers
he recalled and they came from all sides

from the church from behind
from the north and south

The course and temperature of the first greeting
are of utmost significance

to the ultimate fate of any relationship

FROM ABOVE

This journey is like you are going to heaven.
—Lost Boys of Sudan

or you may arrive by helicopter

(a way to kiss over paperwork)

in this form of migration

true or false is

children laugh & slap at water

someone must leave a village

to arrive in a city

first love then bombing

(or, fill in the blanks)

from village to town to _____

turnstile love is a country when _____

on horseback to aim a rifle you must _____

(now, translate into a mother tongue)

from above everything looks _____

& in this manner the river becomes a drum

FAIL TO CONTAIN

Tree lines and stars made of wire
empty field that isn't

Swipe of quiet animals
learning to cross in order

Child in cage image
of child in cage

There is no explaining it
is all part of the explanation

> *In order to what? Or sing*
> *your name when it is your turn*

> *Their there*
> *Their their*

> *There there*
> *They're there*

Official voice imagined room
Testing borders between

rhyme and repetition
Lines form

in favor of the privilege
of song or rubber

stamp on hard wood
kick in teeth

gull's beak story
of time and a mountain

Eventually
eventually: anthem

song sounding of footfall
or muted taps on glass

way to measure time
but no longer reflect it

AN EVENING LINE (II)

All she had to know was the song and she knew where she was.
To get back, she just sang the song in reverse.
—Ann Cameron, *Daughters of a Copper Woman*

In a longed-for imaginary
navigation becomes evolution
story omen, music its own

adversity. This veld
at once tenuous and noble
arrives in verses

on the one neither
orchestral nor geographic
grass as instrument

landscape as song
Here is your invitation
to gather under years

of native ancestry, of aridity
and thorn-scrub, an incanted return
Here the ostinato, holding to

the natural between ear and hear
in the silent, walking breath of a woman
and her one word from which we all descend.

(I) Plum

Erasures or changes are impossible—

The piano line's unsung motive interrupts itself in a need to be ordinary. The aside is new, the scale: taken to be new. Erasures become their own unnatural introduction to the One when need is only valued by the group as escape. *Sugar.*

(ll) Lemon

It is easier to play fast than it is for someone to play slow—

Local evidence or minor opinion, the Now is a one that vanishes under influence.

Your pegged army courts innocence, a nailed indictment to rhythm not unlike applause. This is dope only because of numbers—the cornet a later form of envelope, a release from indeed. Odd is necessary only in the way opinion marks time.

The cornet is nothing but influence emphasized by crescendo. *Drop.*

(lll) Parfait

They made their own sounds and their own movements—

To point to Africa but to run the figure on American instruments, done twice to become its own form, the unsung mirror to Now.

We is not an instrument the way rhythm is not neglect: to go on is to employ story that is more interesting than the Now.

No, the instrument is unsung and the rot is its own talent, created twice for cultural renaming. In redefinition is encouragement, an American emancipation where change is unsung and the instrument is always African.

Movement toward the Now employs neglect and timekeepers.

(IV) Alabama

They were discussing the eternal meaning (Yes) of love—

That afternoon, *that* life, *this* aristocracy: a brief American moment, an attempt at affirmation like saying freedom is innocent or the road is real, merely to open a flood of trying, a flight toward the innocent, the impossible. Experience requires faith when eternity is an exit from sense; every removal ends on the inner road, a tribute to force, or innocent's negative: the respect for Now.

This way out for children of an afternoon in America. Our rich, noble trying, our Now: an afternoon of innocence behind the curtain.

After which, the one becomes your Now.

(V) Psalm

Through the storm and after the rain . . . in all ways and forever—

The privilege of your spiritual art lives like a merciful rain. And so the psalm resolves to be *in,* even when engagement means irresolution and only instruments strike for tenor. In with vibration: rain as vibration, rain as a way to enter contradiction.

Or, the *in* of investment: the supreme instrument becomes love, thankful, a future engineered to be unerring.

Unerringly gracious, not unlike an acknowledgment, should love ever experience love.

NEOWISE

The subject must tap with his hand at each letter A.
—Montreal Cognitive Assessment V7.1

What is the final number for if
person, woman, man, camera, TV

The average forest is a mixture
of scenes. He topples, declines

wounds half a dozen other
trees in his fall, his face

shrunken somehow, the wrinkles
become like lines

drawn in clay. What is the final
number for when arrows

are arranged against arrows
poison against poison, craft against

craft—and probably it will also be seen
why he swathed his face and neck

with fresh sacking. What is the final number
for face, velvet, church, daisy, red

One burrowed into one's body—it was
airless and tight—we all felt happy

but the average has happened before
and it will all happen again. Did anyone see

her give you this note? He nodded
seemed to relax, but he still professes

to love these lines. I confess I have done
as much mischief to them as possible. What is

the final number for when she had gone
he went out through the window

He looked toward the forest. There is
tobacco, salt, iron, rattan, can, ornaments

axes, knives, spears, arrows, adzes
rings. What is the final number for

There was a glow in the sky

SEVENTH SONG OF THE CHILD SOLDIERS

Manifest Song

Not the cotton husks, dried as they are in our
lacquer boxes. Nor the masks—angular

blood casting shadow on the walls
Neither the rabbit skins nor the hats—locks

that stand for love. Not the landscapes (Western?)
torn from the frame—hand-rolled

gold and green gasses of history
Not the roomful of shoes nor the train

that brought them here. Not the hair the straw
the bead-eyes watching again as for justice

No limes, their stinging memory of seas and shaped
progress—no basket of apples—nor the market boys

carrying their weight in salt left to right across the page
to an imagined queen. No plans for the new city

modeled on what we remember of Mogadishu Lübeck Lagos
Phnom Penh Cape Town. Not the chairs helmets violins

sextants spears and so on—nor collections of written clues
unless, of course, unless untrue. It had never been a calculation

of need or destiny, truth be told, and there would be no room
made for it now. No room for the middle passage either

nor the music borne in cells, light as it was, light as it had been
mined, plentiful, held in red handfuls of mud. (Listen here for the catch

the practice of song polished into voiced lies.) No wagons, either
old, of course, and old when all routes from the capital—you understand—

NOTES & ACKNOWLEDGMENTS

Poems from this manuscript first appeared in *Posit Journal, Nomaterialism, 420pus, Cloudbank, 580 Split, Boston Review*'s *What Nature* anthology, *American Letters & Commentary, Fence, Word For/Word, Witness, Interim, Bombay Gin,* and *Can We Have Our Ball Back?* A selection of these poems also appeared in the chapbook *NEOWISE,* published by Trainwreck Press (Canada). My gratitude to the editors for their care and support, particularly Susan Lewis, Carol Ciavonne, Jonathan Minton, Carlos Lara, and John C. Goodman.

My love and deep thanks to Susan Tichy—there at the start, and even before then—and Norma Cole—for the line, the lines, and the light. Thank you also to Gillian Conoley for selecting my manuscript for the 2022 Colorado Prize for Poetry and the team at the Center for Literary Publishing for publishing it.

+++

In order of appearance, notes on source texts and procedures for some of this work:

"No Longer in a Mother Tongue" includes words excavated in constrained procedure from *Secrets,* by Nuruddin Farah (Penguin Books, 1999).

Language used in "Fourth Song of the Child Soldiers" comes entirely from titles of illustration plates in a first edition of *Travels in South Africa, Undertaken at the Request of the Missionary Society,* by missionary explorer John Campbell (printed for the author by T. Rutt; pub. Black and Parry, London, 1815).

"Procession" is composed of language systematically extracted from: *We Wish to Inform You that Tomorrow We Will Be Killed with Our Families: Stories from Rwanda,* by Philip Gourevitch (FSG, 1998) [lines 1–2, 16–17]; *Vermeer in Bosnia,* by Lawrence Weschler (Pantheon, 2004) [4–6]; *Aké,* by Wole Soyinka (Vintage International, 1989) [7–8]; *The Palm-Wine Drinkard and My Life in the Bush of Ghosts,* by Amos Tutuola (Grove Press, 1984) [9–12]; *Speak Rwanda,* by Julian R.

Pierce (Picador, 2000) [12–13]; *The Shadow of the Sun*, by Ryszard Kapuscinski (Vintage International, 2002) [14]; and *Heart of Darkness*, by Joseph Conrad (Bantam Classic, 1981) [16].

"The Light Is Not the Usual Light" borrows words and, occasionally, fragments or phrases from *The Tree Where Man Was Born*, by Peter Matthiessen (Penguin, 1995) [incl. page 20, lines 10–11]; *Modernism, Technology, and the Body: A Cultural Study*, by Tim Armstrong (Cambridge University Press, 1998); *The Uses of Enchantment: The Meaning and Importance of Fairy Tales*, by Bruno Bettelheim (Knopf, 1977); *They Poured Fire on Us from the Sky: The True Story of Three Lost Boys from Sudan*, by Alephonsion Deng, Benson Deng, Benjamin Ajak, and Judy A. Bernstein (PublicAffairs, 2006) [incl. page 17, lines 20–21]; *My Life in the Bush of Ghosts*, by Amos Tutuola (Grove Press, 1984) [incl. page 18, lines 11–12]; *Red Cavalry*, by Isaac Babel (1927) [incl. page 20, lines 15–16]; *The Famished Road*, by Ben Okri (Doubleday, 1991) [incl. page 21, lines 17–18]; and *The Age of Insight: The Quest to Understand the Unconscious in Art, Mind, and Brain, from Vienna 1900 to the Present*, by Eric Kandel (Random House, 2012).

The "A is for ANGOLA" series was constructed following the Analytical Dictionary procedure developed by Noël Arnaud for Oulipo. In the constraint, the letters of a root word form a grid to determine all subsequent words and their specific ordering within each definition.

"Palm-Wine Songs for the Ghost King" borrows occasional phrases from *The Palm-Wine Drinkard*, by Amos Tutuola (Grove Press, 1984); *Where the Heart Beats: John Cage, Zen Buddhism, and the Inner Life of Artists*, by Kay Larson (Penguin, 2012) [page 58, lines 1–6]; *Me Against My Brother: At War in Somalia, Sudan and Rwanda*, by Scott Peterson (Routledge, 2000) [page 59, lines 3–4]; *The Uses of Enchantment: The Meaning and Importance of Fairy Tales*, by Bruno Bettelheim (Knopf, 1977) [page 61, lines 5–7]; *We Wish to Inform You that Tomorrow We Will Be Killed with Our Families: Stories from Rwanda*, by Philip Gourevitch (FSG, 1998) [page 61, lines 10–13]; *Emma's War*, by Deborah Scroggins (Vintage, 2004) [page 61, lines 8–9]; and *The Shadow of the Sun*, by Ryszard Kapuscinski (Vintage International, 2002) [page 61, lines 14–16].

In "Watched for Music": the title "Plum" is derived from "Sugar Plum," written by jazz pianist Bill Evans for his wife. The lexicon is borrowed from the liner notes Evans wrote for Miles Davis's *Kind of Blue*, in which he compares the qualities of jazz improvisation and a particular type of spontaneous Japanese visual art.

The title "Lemon" is derived from "Lemon Drop," composed by George Wallington and brought to prominence by the likes of Woody Herman and Gene Krupa. The poem was written in response/while listening to Krupa's version. The lexicon is borrowed from two texts: a 1943 news article reporting on Krupa's arrest for a marijuana-related incident in San Francisco, and Krupa's words taken from the subsequent trial transcript.

The title "Parfait" is derived from *A Little Max (Parfait),* from the 1980s reissue of the seminal *Money Jungle,* featuring extraordinary and sometimes heated improvisations by Duke Ellington, Charles Mingus, and Max Roach. The song is credited to Roach, who also composed *We Insist!* to mark the hundredth anniversary of Lincoln's Emancipation Proclamation. The lexicon comprises a mix of Roach quotes and writings, especially his comments on Africa and social justice in the United States.

The title "Alabama" comes from John Coltrane's extraordinary *Alabama,* written in response to the 16th Street Baptist Church bombing, in Birmingham, Alabama, in 1963. Coltrane used as his guide the emotional and sonic landscape of Martin Luther King, Jr.'s eulogy for the girls killed in that bombing. In this poem, the lexicon is composed from the same King speech.

The title "Psalm" comes from the fourth movement of John Coltrane's *A Love Supreme.* The lexicon is borrowed from Coltrane's liner notes from the entire *Love Supreme* suite.

"Neowise" references Donald Trump's famous misquote of a question in the Montreal Cognitive Assessment as well as Yevgeny Zamyatin's line "There is no final revolution, no final number." Additional language in the poem arrives from *The Shadow of the Sun,* by Ryszard Kapuscinski (Vintage International, 2002); *In Darkest Africa: Vol II,* by Henry M. Stanley (Charles Scribner's Sons, 1890); and *The Famished Road,* by Ben Okri (Doubleday, 1991).

+++

Final thanks and love to Merel, Emmett, Eliza, and my parents, of course.

This book is set in Calluna and Proxima Nova
by The Center for Literary Publishing
at Colorado State University.

Copyediting by Lauren Furman.
Proofreading by Laura Roth.
Book design and typesetting by Alec Witthohn.
Cover design by Stephanie G'Schwind.
Cover art by Jean Lurssen.
Printing by Books International.